My Lucid Dreaming Way

by Sinan Beratli

Table of Contents

Acknowledgements

I would like to thank my mindfulness meditation instructor Robert Michel from Bromley Mindfulness, Chris Hammond from World-of-Lucid-Dreaming, Ryan Hurd from the Dream Studies Academy and Charlie Morley.

I would also like to thank my family and the publishing company for making this book and my last book possible.

Introduction

My dream practice started when I picked up my first book on astral projection. Ever since then I have researched, tried and tested everything that I could find. I have developed my own practice by observing and testing old and new methods of dreaming. My way is always changing as I never stop learning something new.

I would like to think that I have found the essence of religion itself. I feel that all religions on earth come from dream practice and dream experiences. Many ancient scriptures talk about visions and prophetic dreams. This is my opinion; you do not have to agree with me.

I also believe that the subconscious mind has many answers to questions that every individual seeks. I use dream practice not only for happiness but also to learn from. Dream practice can be good for problem solving. Ancient man used dream practice (dream incubation) to find answers for their very survival.

However you want to use dream practice is up to you. I urge you to develop your own way because what works for me may not work for you. I advise you to explore and find your own path. Feel free to absorb techniques that you may like from this book.

The dreaming body

Through many religions and spiritual movements, I have come to find that there are parts of the anatomy that everybody focuses on: the third eye, the throat, the heart and the lower abdomen.

The third eye

Located between the eyebrows, many people focus on this to do astral projection or, in my opinion, WILD lucid dreaming. I have tried this to no avail but I have had pressures in the head that I did not like.

The throat

According to the Upanishads, this is the dreaming chakra. In Tibetan Buddhism they also visualise the 'AH' syllable as red with petals. I have personally had good results in dreaming by doing a meditation on this point. Before going to sleep, I would visualise cosmic energy (or chi) going into my third eye then down to the base of my throat. I would get a choking sensation, which to some means that the chakra is activated. After feeling this sensation I would sleep and have my dreams, though not lucid dreams.

The heart

I have focused on this but have found that an uncomfortable pressure builds up. I have discarded this practice for this reason. This has not been effective for me.

The lower abdomen

The space two inches below the belly button. Some people call this the *dan tien*. This is where cosmic energy (or chi) is stored. Some people visualise storing chi in the perineum. I cannot help thinking that chi practice is an important part of dreaming. I have not focused on this point to do lucid dreaming, just during chi practice.

The importance of the right food

It is very hard to stay healthy since there is fast food everywhere. I admit that I am terrible when it comes to not eating healthily. I like to eat, especially eating out. I understand, however, that aphrodisiac confections are the best thing to eat as sexual energy is important especially for dream practice. So here is the list.

Barley

Lentils or dal

Shilajit

Olive oil

Pistachio nuts

Almonds

Pomegranate

Tasampa or powdered barley

Dates

Honey

Ginseng

Black seeds

Figs

Gogi berries

Avocado

Banana

Ginseng shots

Yerba mate

If you find more then feel free to add them to your diet.

Using herbs and psychedelics

There is a particular way I ingest herbs (or herbs of this nature) if not intimidated or doubtful about them. You do not have to take these substances to do lucid dreaming – the waking practices are really all you need – but again this is what I do. If you choose to do it, proceed at your own risk. I strongly advise you not to take psychedelic herbs if you suffer from mental illness and to keep clear from lucid dreaming altogether.

Another note: I only take these to relax me, not to hallucinate. In my opinion, this is how you use these herbs properly. I am not responsible for anything that happens. Having said that, this is how I take herbs of this nature.

Psychedelic laci

1 teaspoon of herb of your choice

1 tablespoon of yogurt

1 cup of milk

1 half an orange or ¼ glass of fruit juice

Making the laci

1.   Brew the herb 2–3 minutes or until it gets cold. Use a tea strainer and one small cup of boiling water.

2.   Mix the yogurt, milk and juice together in a glass but do not fill it.

3.   Pour however much of the brewed mixture in the glass to fill it and there you have it – the psychedelic laci.

This is an inspiration from the bang laci that the Hindus make with cannabis.

Below is a list of herbs that have been widely used in the lucid dreaming community.

Calea zachatechi

Heimia salicifolia

Silene capensis

Mugwort

Burdock

Blue lotus

Ayahuasca

Wild Asparagus Root

Mullein

Celastrus Paniculatus

The importance of saving sexual energy

According to Esoteric Christianity, conserving your sexual energy at the right times of the lunar cycle makes you produce melatonin, serotonin and DMT. These are lucid-dreaming chemicals and are important for every lucid dreamer.

Bear in mind that most, if not all, religions preach celibacy and no masturbation. I think we all now know why! Also, many religious and spiritual sects say that the dream realm is the death, or spiritual, realm.

Chi cultivation

When it comes to gathering energy, I usually do this in the morning before sunrise when I have time. These exercises are a mixture of Taoist movements and pranyama breathing from the Hindu faith.

Start off by doing basic pranyama breathing by closing your right nostril with your thumb and breathing in through your left nostril. Close your left nostril with your ring finger, release your right nostril and breathe out. Now breathe in through your right nostril, close it with your thumb, then release your ring finger and breathe out of your left nostril. Do this three times.

After doing this, breathe through both nostrils in and out three times.

I do the next set of exercises in any order.

1)   Run your tongue over your teeth ten times, swish your saliva around (like mouthwash) then swallow.

2)   Turn your head to your left, then right, then bring back to the centre. Do this three times.

3)   Using the index fingers of both hands, place them on the back of your skull where the neck meets the back of your head. Flick your index fingers so they hit the base of the skull where the neck and skull meet. Do this by placing the index fingers on the middle fingers and pushing them down to generate the flick effect. Do this thirty times.

4)   Open and close your mouth so that your teeth strike together. Do this with your

mouth closed. Do not strike too hard. Do this thirty times

5) Bring your hands to the centre of your body, palms facing upwards. Interlock your fingers, breathe in, then raise your hands with your hands facing out as if you are pushing the ceiling away. When your arms reach their full extent, breathe out. Turn to the left and right, then bring your arms back to where you started. Do this three times.

6) Repeat exercise number 5 but instead of pushing up, push down and turn. Do this three times. (Do not interlock your fingers.)

7) Start as for exercise number 6, but this time simultaneously push to the sky with your right hand and push to the ground with your left hand. Breathe out on the outward push of the hands. Do this three times, then alternate with your right hand pushing towards the ground and the left hand towards the sky. No turning is required for this exercise.

8) Sway from left to right three times.

9)   Rub your chin with the palm of your hand thirty times.

10)   Rub your hands together until hot, then massage your kidneys. Do this three times.

11)   As you breathe in, visualise air coming in through your fingertips and toes so that it covers the whole of your skeleton. Breathe out, visualising the air coming out of your fingertips and toes. Some people call this 'bone marrow breathing'.

The importance of meditation

The only meditation that I do is mantra meditation. I feel that this is best because it helps you still your mind.

I have read that meditation for an hour before bed heightens your chances of having a lucid dream. Another form of meditation I practise is placing my attention on the bottom of my nose where the air goes in and out. The choice is yours according to what meditation you prefer, as everybody is different.

Fasting

I have found that fasting is a good way of getting into a trance sleepy state. I have read in a book, *Creative Dreaming* by Patricia Garfield, that Native Americans use fasting when incubating a dream to speak to a deity. This is, of course, optional.

The importance of mindfulness

Mindfulness meditation and waking exercises I feel is very important as it helps you exercise awareness and absorption of the now and present. Observation and attention of everything you touch, feel, taste, see and hear is important for lucid dreaming. I have personally found that my dreams have become more clearer and realistic when I practice mindfulness. Combining that clarity with reality checks produces results I assure you.

My method of lucid dreaming

Here I will share with you my way of dreaming practice. Feel free to absorb from this as I have absorbed from many others.

Waking practice

Reality check

A reality check is when you question whether you are dreaming or not dreaming and perform a test to prove it. A typical example is that you ask yourself if you're dreaming then try to push your finger through your hand. If your hand goes through, you are obviously dreaming; if not, then you're not dreaming.

I have found that simply asking the question and looking around has given me results by itself, but I have developed my own method of reality checking as you will see in the next pages.

Different modes

There are three modes that I shift to throughout the day: the non-interactive mode, interactive mode, and the last resort mode.

The first mode is used in the relaxed state – walking, jogging, waiting in a queue, etc. While in this mode I am keeping my attention on my five senses and my mantra. In this mode I have nothing on my mind.

The second mode is used when I interact, for example at work, or with people, or doing something that involves mental thought, or general interaction with my surroundings. When I am in this mode, I keep my attention on my five senses and do a reality check whenever I can.

The last resort mode is for when I am not able to use the other modes and am going through a very, very tough time. I say to myself, 'Please tell me I am dreaming right now,' and do a reality check.

If I am having a bad day in general, I give reality checks a break. If I am having a stressful period dealing with life problems, I tend to find that my reality checking gets to an all-time low because I'm thinking of the problems at hand.

The mantra

The mantra is something I have developed myself using different syllables. I urge you to develop your own if you do not like mine.

The way I developed my mantra is by observing many different mantras, extracting the most commonly-used syllables and using them to create my own. These syllables are *ah, i, m, ta, sha, la, ra, na, sa,* and *pa.*

I liked the sound of A, as *ah* or *A* is in many religions, but my mantra has no meaning behind it as I am not spiritual or religious. The mantra is made up of five main syllables which are then reversed to make ten syllables in total. You will also notice that I have switched the letters of the syllables above around. If you look at my mantra you will see what I mean.

Aht Ahn Ahp Ahc Aha Aha Ahc Ahp Ahn Aht.

I use this mantra when I am in mode one, so I am basically doing a reality check every ten seconds. When I mentally say the mantra, each syllable should last a second.

It goes like this: Aht Ahn Ahp Ahc Aha Aha Ahc Ahp Ahn Aht … at this point, you can look around you and ask if you are dreaming or you can do other physical reality checks.. Mantras and reality checks are done mentally.

Here is a word of advice: mastering your chosen mantra takes time … mine did! It was an absolute tongue twister but I soon got the hang of it. I can now say it mentally effortlessly.

Lucid triggers

Start with your mind; if you're thinking of something annoying or negative, ask yourself if you're dreaming then observe your surroundings. Mindfulness is important for lucid dreaming as it exercises awareness.

I have found it a common problem that I forget to do a reality check, not just because of life stresses but mainly because of my thoughts. I tend to daydream a lot, which is not good for dreaming. To solve this problem, I made it a habit to ask myself if I was dreaming every time I daydreamed. If I have bad or angry thoughts, I use the flaw of my overactive mind to ask myself if I am dreaming. Your mind will be different to mine, but experiment and observe your mind to see what works for you. Then observe your life and see when you can do a reality check. These are called lucid triggers.

If you observe the surroundings of your everyday life, you will find there are many you can use. Here is a list of some:

- When you walk through a door

- When you see someone

- When you type or write

- When you touch your Oyster card on a reader

- When you see your bus coming up the road

… the list goes on.

It is understandably different for everybody since we all live different lives.

While reading

Keep attention on your five senses. Ask yourself before your read, during reading or at the end of the page or paragraph. Do whatever you can do in the moment. If this type of concentration is not possible for whatever reason, then do a check whenever and however much you can.

Writing

A check can be done before writing, during writing or after you have written. Again, if you cannot maintain this concentration for whatever reason, then do a reality check whenever you can.

Listening

A reality check can be done before someone talks, while

the person is talking and after he/she has talked. Again, if you cannot maintain this concentration for whatever reason, then do a reality check whenever you can while keeping attention on the five senses. While listening to music, I focus on my five senses as much as I can. I do a reality check roughly every ten seconds when listening to music.

Gaming

I am a very big gamer and find that I cannot do a reality check, especially if I am playing competitively. I find that I can do checks when I am playing alone with no stress.

There are other types of reality check you can do randomly throughout the day These are the extra things you can do:

- Try to move objects with your mind

- Try to put your hand through solid objects

- Push your finger into your hand

- Try to float through the ceiling with your mind

- Try to breathe through your pinched nose

- Try to change writing or signs with your mind

- Stare and observe objects for a long time

- Pull your finger

- Look at your nose with one eye closed.

Some reality checks are taught by our own dreams. I will give you an example of a dream that I had.

I am eating with a man. Before I put the food in my mouth he stops me. He then tells me to ask if I am dreaming. I do as he commands. I put the food in my mouth and he again commands me to ask if I am dreaming. I ask again, as he commanded, then I wake up.

Not all dreams show you as directly as this.

A word of advice: you must practise reality checks so they become a habit. This takes time, so do not be discouraged if you do not do the reality checks properly for a few months.

Sleeping postures

Posture 1

This posture is done by sleeping on your side with your right hand underneath your cheek and your left arm on your left side. This posture is practised in Buddhism dream practice. They say that a man should sleep on his right side and a woman should sleep on her left side. They believe that the positive and negative sides of the male and female are opposite, and the positive is on the right side in man but the left side in women. I have found this posture to be very comfortable but have found that my private parts gets crushed, so I have to 'readjust' myself.

I have also found in the Sahi Bukari that Mohamed, the prophet, told his followers that it is best to sleep on their right side. I have read in one of Carlos Castaneda's books that he was told to sleep on his right side. I cannot remember which book it was but I urge you to read all of them. You will like them – I promise lots of laughs.

Position 2

This position is the similar to the last one, the only difference is that the left leg is stretched out.

The position is a variation of the previous sleeping position. I find that this does not crush my private parts but the left side of the ribcage overstretches, which can be uncomfortable. I found out through research into Taoist sleep practices that this is very similar to the sleeping-dragon pose, which was adopted by the Taoist sage Chen Tuan. Read 'Life and teaching of two immortals : Chen Tuan volume 2 by Hua- Ching Ni if you're interested.

Position 3

This position is same as Position 2 but with the left hand on the right bicep. This sleeping posture is more comfortable than the last one, as I place my left hand on my bicep but my left ribcage still stretches.

Position 4

In this position you are on your belly with your right arm straight by your side and your left knee bent at a ninety-degree angle. The left arm is also bent at a ninety-degree angle with your hand beside your head and the palm facing down. This is my favourite sleeping position; I have had many spiritual experiences in this position. Again, experiment with all the positions described to find which is most comfortable for you.

Sleeping practice

There are 3 types of practice that I have invented for going to sleep, I have invented this for Dream incubation, WILD lucid dreaming and astral projection. In all honesty I have not experimented with these particular techniques yet so I do not know if they work, but I will share anyway just in case it may work for you. I also would like to point out that I have added the astral projection practice as I would like to experiment and find out myself if astral projection and WILD lucid dreaming is the same. I think it is, but would like to make certain of this claim, so I will be experimenting with these myself. These techniques involve using the mantra that I have developed (your own developed mantra can be used)

Dream Incubation

The mantra would go like this if you want to incubate about someone or a question:

Aht.....Ask question/say someone's name Ahn....Ask question/say someone's name Ahp...Ask question/say someone's name Ahc... Ask question/say someone's name Aha... Ask question/say someone's name Aha... Ask question/say someone's name Ahc Ask question/say someone's name Ahp....Ask question/say someone's name Ahn...Ask question/say someone's name Aht...Ask question/say someone's name

You repeat this as your falling asleep, if you forget what syllable you are on you start from the beginning.

WILD Lucid dreaming

Aht..... I am dreaming Ahn.... I am dreaming Ahp... I am dreaming Ahc... I am dreaming Aha... I am dreaming Aha... I am dreaming   Ahc I am dreaming Ahp.... I am dreaming Ahn... I am dreaming   Aht... I am dreaming

You repeat this as your falling asleep, if you forget what syllable you are on you start from the beginning.

Astral projection

It is advisable to master WILD lucid dreaming before doing astral projection just in case there is such thing as soul separation but I still think it's the same thing because some people say it is different, and if it is different we all need to be very careful with this one! The technique is exactly the same as the WILD practice however your intent is to get out of the body. So you say out of the body between every syllable. Like this.

Aht…Out the body Ahn…out the body Ahp…out the body Ahc…out the body Aha… out the body Aha…out the body Ahc..out the body Ahp…out the body Ahn.. out the body Aht…out the body.

Waking-up practice

After you have had your dream and slept, get into the habit of keeping your eyes closed and your body still. Also run through your dreams seven times in your mind. I find this technique to be really effective in developing dream recall.

The most important bit of the waking-up practice is to write down your dreams in a dream diary. If you do not have time to lie still and to go through your dreams seven times, just write down what you remember, no matter how little.

Dream journaling

Writing in your dream journal can be a tricky thing.

Some days you remember dreams; some days I have found you do not. If you do not, do not worry about it. Just keep on doing reality checks and eventually you will have a lucid dream.

I will also share with you how I fill out my journal. There are many authors who tell you to sketch, write the time, give your dream a title, etc. I have found this to be very impractical but you can give it a try – maybe you'll be able to do it.

The way I write my dream journal is very simple: I write down the date then sleep. I tend to wake up many times during the night or day, depending on if I have done a night shift or not. The first dream I have, I simply write the number 1, circle it, then write the dream down. I always write in present tense.

If I then go back to bed and have another dream, I do the same thing again: number 2, circle it, write it down. If my dream was lucid then I put a star next to the number or a capital L with a circle around it.

I am a very light sleeper so I tend to get up at least two or three times a night. There are times when I get up, remember the dream but cannot be bothered to write it down. It can't be helped – we all do it. Just write in your diary 'Did not have time' or 'Forgot to dream'.

Dream signs

Dream signs are basically things that you do not see in your waking state. For example, if you see a celebrity in your dream you know after waking up that it was only a dream. The good thing is that your dream teaches you your own dream signs to look out for. I will give you an example from my dream.

I walk into my mother's bedroom and see three cats lying down on her bed. I think nothing of it and carry on listening to my mother talking.

I wake up thinking I should have known that this was a dream because we have only two cats in our household. This was a long time ago, as now the family has three cats in the house. I also tend to see my parents often in my dreams so that is another reality check for me.

Final thoughts

I hope this has helped you, the reader, to have lucid

dreams. I feel that more of us should be practising lucid dreaming, as this ability is being forgotten as time goes on. It is a good ability to have; many great minds have used their dreams to aid their creativity.

Teachers

I would like to thank the following teachers for teaching me their methods of peace, worship and happiness. If you are interested, I have listed their contact details below. I urge everybody to learn from them

<u>Bromley Mindfulness</u>

Robert Mitchell   0759048993

<u>www.bromleymindfulness.org.uk</u>

<u>Dream Studies Academy (Lucid Ignition workshop)</u>
Ryan Hurd

<u>world-of-lucid-dreaming</u> Chris Hammond

Charlie Morley   <u>www.charliemorley.com</u>

References

http://www.dlshq.org/download/download.htm

Tenzin Wangyal Rinpche, *Tibetan Yogas of Dream and Sleep*, Snow Lion Publications, 1998

Alan Wallace, *Dreaming Yourself Awake*, Publications Inc, 2012

Dylan Tuccillo, Jared Zeizel and Thomas Peisel, *A Field Guide to Lucid Dreaming*, Workman Publishing, 2010

David M. Jinks, *How to Control Your Dreams: 79 techniques tips and tricks*, Glass Moon Press, 2011

Rebecca Turner, *The Art of Lucid Dreaming*, Creative Media NZ Ltd, 2011

Lucid Dreaming Techniques, Lionshare Media, 2014

Sergio Magana Ocelocoyotol, *The Toltec Secret*, Hay House UK Ltd, 2014

Samael Aun Weor, *Dream Yoga*, Glorian Publishing, 2010

Daniel Love, *Are you Dreaming?,* Enchanted Loom

Publishing, 2013

Jonas Ridgeway, *Exploring Your Inner Reality*, 2016

Phyllis L. Pipitone, PhD, *The Inner World of Dreams*,
Supreme Grand Lodge of the Ancient and Mystical Order
Roses Crucis, 2015

Robert Wagganer & Caroline McCready, *Lucid Dreaming*,
Conari Press, 2015

Patricia L. Garfield, *Creative Dreaming*, Firesie, 1995

Steven Laberge & Howard Rheingold, *Exploring the
World of Lucid Dreaming*, Ballantine Books,1994

Robert Waggoner, *Lucid Dreaming*, Moment Point Press
Inc, 2008

Sri Aurobindo, *The Yoga of Sleep and Dreams*, Ashram
Press, 2004

Castaneda Carlos, *The Teachings of Don Juan: A Yaqui
Way of Knowledge*, Penguin Books,1968

Castaneda Carlos, *The Second Ring of Power*, A
Touchstone Book, 1977

Castaneda Carlos , *The Fire from Within*, Black Swan Books, 1984

Castaneda Carlos, *Magical Passes*, HarperCollins Publishers, 1998

Castaneda Carlos, *The Wheel of Time*, Washington Square Press, 1998

Castaneda Carlos, *The Active Side of Infinity*, Laugan Productions, 1998

Carlos Castaneda, *The Eagles Gift* , Pocket Books/ Washington Square Press, 1981

Taisha Abelar, *The Sorcerer's Crossing: a Woman's Journey*, Penguin Group, 1992

Carlos Castaneda's *Tensegrity Vol 1,2,3*,Terra Entertainment DVD, 2004

Will Adcock, Rosalind Powell, Laura J. Watts, *Dream Power & Shaman Energy*, Anness Publishing, 2001

Sri Aurobindo, *The Integral Yoga*, Lutus Press, 1993

Cunningham Scott, *Dreaming the Divine*, Llewellyn Worldwide Ltd, 2016

Keith Harary & Pamela Weintraub, *Lucid Dreams in 30 Days: the creative sleep program*, St Martin's Griffin, 1989

Keith Harary & Pamela Weintraub, *Have an Out-of-Body Experience in 30 Days*, Thorsons, 1995

Paul & Charla Devereux, *Lucid Dreaming: accessing your inner virtual realties*, Daily Grail Publishing, 1998

Ted Andrews, *Dream Alchemy*, Llewellyn Publications, 2015

Stephen Larsen, *The Transformational Power of Dreaming*, Larsen and Verner, 2017

Jeremy Jameson, *Lucid Dreaming*, 9591451canada Inc, 2016

Stefan Z , *5 Steps to Lucid Dreaming*, HowtoLucid.com, 2015

Dagny Walters, *Lucid Dreaming for Beginners*, 2015

Paul Kain, *Lucid Dreaming*, 2016

Ryan Hurd, *Lucid*, DreamStudies Press, 2012

Jason Thomas, *The 100 Most Powerful Affirmations for Lucid Dreaming*, WorldAffirmations.com, 2016

Slider, *The WILD to Lucid Dreaming*, Lonebird Publications, 2016

Mark Stavish, LLC *Between the Gates*, Red Wheel/Weiser, 2008

Arnold Mindell, *Dreaming while Awake*, Hampton Roads Publishing Company Inc., 2000

Ryan Hurd and Kelly Bulkeley, *Lucid Dreaming*, Library of Congress Cataloging-in- Publication Data, 2014

Michael Raduga, *A practical guidebook for lucid dreaming and out of body travel*, www.obe4u.com, 2011

Clare R. Johnson PhD, *Complete Book of Lucid Dreaming*, Llewellyn Publications, 2017

Clare R. Johnson PhD, *Mindful Dreaming*, Conari Press, 2018

Thomas Yuschak, *Advanced Lucid Dreaming*, AdvancedLD. Lt, 2006

Richard Bullivant, *Lucid Dreaming Health, Wealth and*

Prosperity, 2014

The Lucid Dreaming Handbook, Golden Ink Publishing, 2015

Dayanara Blue Star, *Exploring the World of Lucid Dreaming,* J.D. Rockefeller, 2015

Daniel Allen Kelley, *Behind the veil,* The Original Falcon Press, 2018

Frederick Aardema, *A New Approach to Out of Body Experiences,* Mount Royal Publishing, 2012

Pamela Ball, *Lucid Dreaming,* Arcturus Publishing, 2011

Lucid Dreaming & Access Your Past Lives, Hypnosis Enterprises, 2017

William Hart, *The Art of Living Vipassana Meditation,* Pariyatti Publishing, 1987

Daniel Love, *Lucid The Tao of Dreaming,* Enchanted Loom Publishing, 2018

Mark McElroy, *Lucid Dreaming for Beginners,* Llewellyn Publications, 2007

Victoria Socolova, *How to Get to Lucid Dream,* Magickum, 2016

Edain McCoy, *Astral Projection for Beginners,* Llewellyn publications, 1999

Charlie Morley, *Lucid Dreaming Made Easy,* Hay House UK Ltd, 2018

Nico Klingler, *Lucid Dreaming Made Easy,* Grin, 2018

Kenneth Kelzer, *The Sun and the Shadow,* A.R.E Press,1987

Jamie Alexander, *Teach Your Child how to Lucid Dream,* lucidAbility.com, 2013

Lisa Shea, *Lucid Dreaming Guide,* LisaShea.com, 2004–2015

Tabitha Zalot, *New Age Bundle 2 Astral Projection Lucid Dreaming,* Lean Stone Publishing, 2017

Craig Hamilton-Parker, *Dream Book Trilogy No 1 Lucid dreaming and Dream Recall,* Sterling Publishing, 2000

Shark Bite Coaching, *Intentional Dreaming*, Playful publications, 2013

Nicolas Cato Strode, *Strodes Guide to Mysticism,* Ovasol Industries, 2015

Case Adams, *The Science of the Dreaming,* logicalbooks, 2014

John A. McClain, *Mastering Lucid Dreams in 7 Days,* First Printing, 2012

AJ Clarke, *How to Lucid Dream in 7 Days or Less!,* Spartus Group, 2012

S Rob, *Secrets of Lucid Dreaming Revealed,* Castindes Publishing, 2014

Himani Vashishta, *Out of Body Experience & Lucid Dreaming,* Astral Projection, Unicorn Books, 2016

Tony Crisp, *Lucid Dreaming,* Octopus Publishing Group, 2006

Teresa Martin, *Lucid Dreaming,* SOM Publishing, 2008

Jurgen Ziewe, *Multidimensional Man,* www.lightmagic.co.uk 2008

Tom Bisio, *Daoist Sleeping Meditation,* Outskirts Press, 2018

Alex Master, *Lucid Dreaming Techniques,* Play Magic Publisher

Ian Wilson, *You Are Dreaming,* Amazon Kindle Edition, 2019

Olga Kharitid MD, *Master of Lucid Dream*, Hampton Roads Publishing Company Inc, 2001

Professor Jerry Alan Johnson PHD, *Daoist Magical Transformation Skills,* The International Institute of Medical Qigong Publishing House, 2012

Jennifer Dumpert, *Liminal Dreaming,* North Atlantic Books, 2019

Patricia Smith, *Lucid Dreaming,* Conscious Living Media, 2019

Alicia Leigh, *The Dreaming Writer,* www.fallinlovewithleigh.com, 2018

John Lockley, *Leopard Warrior*, Sounds True Malidoma Some, 2017

Zainurrahman, *Lucid Dreaming, how to enter someone's dream*, Z&F Self-Publishing and Store, 2019

.